Reviews of Jason's earlier works

I thoroughly enjoyed *Christian Sex Today*! I particularly enjoyed and laughed out loud at the summary of an Old Testament sexual ethic – a real warning against judgmentalism! To find polyamory being explored in a book about Christian sexuality was an eye opener! I found it extremely helpful in terms of how to talk about sex to my daughter when she's older, especially given the unhelpful conservative framework I grew up with.   Rachel Collis Performer

With flashes of humour and much deep thought, the author takes us, time and again, on a journey from the origins of a belief system to its inappropriate current-day application.   Dr Miriam Verbeek

I'm Not a Racist But is nothing you'd expect to read from a church minister but everything you've ever wanted one to say. Addressing politics, sex and religion with thought-provoking humour, this unorthodox collection makes no apologies for its audacious, controversial and challenging poems. Be prepared for your religious stereotypes to be smashed wide open in the most refreshing of ways. Jason John is, without a doubt, the Australian Pete Holmes.

Also by Jason John

Worshipping Evolution's God

A Walk in the Park

I'm Not a Racist, but I've got a Racist Butt
(poetry collection)

Christian Sex Today:
Lessons from Moses, Paul, Jesus and Darwin

ecofaith.org

Easter Horror Stories

Rescuing Jesus' Good News

Jason John

Copyright 2021, all rights reserved.

ISBN: (paperback) 978-0-6488257-3-9

ISBN: (ebook) 978-0-6488257-2-2

The right of Jason John to be identified as the author of this book has been asserted by him in accordance with the *Copyright Amendment (Moral Rights) Act 2000.*

This work is copyright as spelt out in the Australian Copyright Act 1968.

All other use requires the prior written permission of Jason John, via jasonrobertjohn@gmail.com

Cover image: DALL-E

This book uses the 'New Revised Standard Version Bible, copyright 1989, Division of Christian Education of the National Council of the Churches of Christ in the United States of America. Used by permission. All rights reserved.' In all cases where there are italics, they have been added by the author.

Contents

Introduction — 12

Lent 1 (Feb 18, 2024) — 17
Salvation for Noah and his sons.

Lent 2 (Feb 25, 2024) — 39
Salvation for the Jews.

Lent 3 (March 3, 2024) — 39
Salvation for *obedient, merciless* Jews.

Lent 4 (March 10, 2024) — 51
Salvation for *compliant* Jews.

Lent 5 (March 17, 2024) — 63
Spiritual Communism:
Jeremiah and Jesus

Lent 6 (March 24, 2024) 76
Salvation outside the Temple

Maundy Thursday (March 28) 86
Bad things happen to good people.
Even Jesus.

Friday (March 29, 2024) 91
There is nothing good about it.

Resurrection Sunday (March 31) 93
The world's first cliff-hanger.

Dedication

To Matthew, who took the time to tell me personally that he appreciated the book, and preferred the original title, to which I've reverted.

To Finn and Scout, to whom I read a slightly censored version of the first draft at bed-time, all the way back in 2009! Thanks for your encouragement and insight, and optimism at how many copies I might sell, and how rich it might make you. Though to your credit - and luckily – you thought it more important to write books worth reading, than to make money out of them.

Invitation

2024 is the year of Mark in the Revised Common Lectionary, a set of suggested readings from the bible, which is used by churches around the world. So I'm working on a way that people who are excited by the themes and ideas in the book can discuss them together, either live online or through a chat forum. You can always come to the conversation late if it is 2027 or even 2030, when Mark is back in the lectionary again.

Or if you are lucky enough to be part of an in person small group, there are questions scattered throughout the chapters, which will hopefully generate discussion.

Join the conversation or get the questions from **ecofaith.org**

Introduction

Easter is coming! Rescue, healing, wholeness, death and Resurrection...

Salvation!

But what does salvation mean, how does it work, who is it for, and what has it got to do with Jesus, whoever he is?

Churches around the world read stories of salvation from the Hebrew Scriptures in the lead up to Easter, and connect them to stories of Jesus, especially his murder and the Resurrection.

The specific stories we read are set down in a lectionary, so that most churches around the world are reading the same stories each week. That is a beautiful thing, or it would be, except that most of the stories chosen are horrible.

Inevitably, some kinds of people get saved, and others get left out. Someone is always rescued *at the expense* of someone else.

The stories we read are not so much "love your neighbour" stories, as "be glad you aren't your neighbour" stories.

There was winners and losers, God's team and the other team. These stories feature God as a violent, genocidal maniac, rightly troubling anyone who allows themselves to be troubled by what they read in the biblical witnesses.

In 2024, the lectionary focuses on Marks' gospel, and this book follows those readings, so that you can read the book in parallel to attending worship, and perhaps discuss it in a study group.

I hope that in challenging these "us and them" stories in the Bible, we might also challenge them as they are repeated over and over again in secular versions around the world. The tension between "us and them" isn't restricted to the religious sphere. There are always relatively well-off people being encouraged by the

Powers that Be, to be thankful that we are not our neighbour, and to not rock the boat too much in case we ruin the economy or lose our funding and *become* our poor neighbour.

As a new Christian in my twenties, these stories horrified me, yet I felt compelled to "believe them," since they were part of the package. I fervently hoped that there was some mysterious divine explanation for their overt xenophobia and control by fear approach to questioning authority. Usually, I just glossed over the bad bits like everyone else seemed to, because after all the Spirit really did seem to be active amongst the people who believed all this stuff, or at least who said they believed it.

Eventually I came to see that the biblical witnesses are a collection of arguments about the nature of God and humanity, not a monolithic or coherent thesis. We can contrast, for example, the xenophobia of much of the Old Testament with the books of Ruth (where a foreigner becomes the ancestor of David) and Jonah (who sulks when God cares about foreigners and is sternly rebuked).

In passing, I want to acknowledge that of course Judaism contained and contains a multitude of relationships to the scriptures, foreigners, women and so on. I am not setting out to contrast Christianity, or Jesus, with "Judaism" or criticising Judaism. What I am criticising is the uncritical way in which the Church picks up many stories of salvation in the Hebrew Scriptures, or Old Testament, and repeats them in the lectionary and therefore in worship, even if occasionally censoring out the most horrible bits. We repeat stories of winners and losers, featuring a xenophobic, abusive God, as if they are a part of our story.

So now let us work through Lent in the lectionary, to frankly examine the horrific Old Testament stories, in parallel with the stories of Jesus being read around the churches. Let us see what Jesus, and the Hebrew prophets who inspired him, made of those stories.

Then we will arrive at Maundy Thursday, bad Friday, and finally Easter Sunday, asking not so much what the Resurrection *was*, but what it *means*.

Spoiler alert: it means salvation. But how does this salvation work, who is it for, and what has it got to do with Jesus, whoever he is? Does Jesus support, fulfil, or undermine the stories we are hearing in the Hebrew Scriptures?

We will see that Jesus and the gospel writers had different answers to those questions than Paul and some other early Christian writers. And, indeed, to most Christians today.

The chapters are dated according to the readings in the Revised Common Lectionary, but you can read them whenever you like!

Lent 1 (Feb 18, 2024)

Salvation for Noah and his sons.

Genesis 9:8-17
Psalm 25:1-10
1 Peter 3:18-22
Mark 1:9-15

The Genesis 9 reading is the one where God promises never again to flood the Earth and destroy all life on it.

All around the world, churches who follow the lectionary will be engaging with this story. The lectionary bit is lovely. Around 40% of Australian Christians take this story of the flood and Noah's survival historically. Even those who do not, usually celebrate it as a lovely message, a sign that God is trustworthy and good. God promises never to hurt us again, no matter how bad we get, at least by flood,

> Then God said to Noah and to his sons with him, "As for me, I am establishing my Covenant with you and your descendants after you, and with every living creature that is with you, the birds, the domestic animals, and every animal of the earth with you, as many as came out of the ark. I establish my Covenant with you, that never again shall all flesh be cut off by the waters of a flood, and never again shall there be a flood to destroy the earth." God said, "This is the sign of the Covenant that I make between me and you and every living creature that is with you, for all future

generations: I have set my bow in the clouds, and it shall be a sign of the Covenant between me and the earth. When I bring clouds over the earth and the bow is seen in the clouds, I will remember my Covenant that is between me and you and every living creature of all flesh; and the waters shall never again become a flood to destroy all flesh. When the bow is in the clouds, I will see it and remember the everlasting Covenant between God and every living creature of all flesh that is on the earth." God said to Noah, "This is the sign of the Covenant that I have established between me and all flesh that is on the earth." (Genesis 9:8-17)

Ecologically minded Christians are thrilled to point out that *all* flesh, *all* life is included in the Covenant! But let us read the *preface* to this story, which isn't in the lectionary,

> "God blessed Noah and his sons, and said to them, "Be fruitful and multiply, and fill the earth. *The fear and dread of you shall rest on every animal of the earth*, and on every bird of the air, on

everything that creeps on the ground, and on all the fish of the sea; *into your hand they are delivered.* Every moving thing that lives shall be food for you; and just as I gave you the green plants, *I give you everything.*" (Genesis 9:1-3)

So, the salvation of humans requires the dread and enslavement of *all other life*! God only cares about humans, and treats other animals as mere objects. Even worse, if we read closely, we see that it is only *Noah and his sons* who are blessed and given everything.

Can it get any worse? Certainly!

Why is God promising never to kill all flesh by flood again? Because God just *did* kill all flesh, as we read earlier in the story,

> "The LORD saw that the wickedness of humankind was great in the earth, and that every inclination of the thoughts of their hearts was only evil continually. And the LORD was sorry that he had made humankind on the earth, and it grieved him to his heart.

So the LORD said, "I will blot out from the earth the human beings I have created -- people together with animals and creeping things and birds of the air, for I am sorry that I have made them." (Genesis 6:5-7)

God is a mass murderer. Killing almost all life, apparently because humans are evil, except for Noah. This next bit isn't in the Bible, but we can imagine this is how it would have looked,

"So God sent floods upon the Earth, and after forty days the stench of decay was upon the water. Vacantly staring babies and pregnant women, their foetuses now still within their wombs. Newborn lambs and once faithful hounds. The infirm, the senile, mighty elephants and tiny worms. All joined in a stinking raft of rotting flesh, islands upon which the carrion birds rested, and below which estuarine fish feasted."

God saved Noah by mass murdering babies. God commits a global abortion on a scale beyond the worst nightmares of pro-life advocates. The bible does not condemn killing unborn babies if God does it. Not only that, but billions of life forms who apparently are not evil, or even smart enough to be evil, are murdered too.

Is this the God we worship?

Is this the God we love?

Could we ever trust that this God loves us?

Genesis 9 offers salvation - assurance of God's protection - for humans (men) at the expense of all other life. And the kind of God who offers that protection is the kind of God who just committed mass genocide and ecocide.

We cannot divorce the rainbow, the nice message offered in the lectionary, from the rest of the story. I hope we will not accept the flood story. Thank God that evolution gives us a strong basis for rejecting it literally.

Hopefully, I have convinced you to reject it metaphorically. It is nothing but bad news for all life except a few men.

I wonder if exposing and rejecting this story might help us expose and reject other stories. Have powerful men or women in our lives convinced us that we need to be punished, and that they have the right to mete out that punishment? Have they been violent to us and promised not to hurt us again, as long as we don't upset them? Have they claimed that we ought to be grateful that they have promised not to hurt us again, or that they have selected us as favourites whilst assaulting others. Have we felt grateful that it wasn't us who got walloped, and therefore not spoken up in protest so it didn't *become* us?

Or have we looked on as the world "drowns" in debt, and been thankful that we are on *Ark Australia*, which appears to be relatively watertight for now? Have we congratulated ourselves on our obvious righteousness at not sinking?

Meanwhile, in Jesus' adventure this week, we have him entering the Outback to get a clear head,

"In those days Jesus came from Nazareth of Galilee and was baptized by John in the Jordan. And just as he was coming up out of the water, Jesus saw the heavens torn apart and the Spirit descending like a dove on him. And a voice came from heaven, "You are my Son, the Beloved; with you I am well pleased." Then the Spirit immediately drove him out into the wilderness. He was in the wilderness forty days, tempted by Satan; and he was with the wild beasts; and the angels waited on him.

Now after John was arrested, Jesus returned to Galilee, proclaiming the good news of God, and saying, "The time is fulfilled, and the Kingdom of God has come near. Repent and believe in the good news." (Mark 1:9-15)

What an overwhelming way to discover who you are!

In Mark, Jesus discovers who he is at his baptism- the beloved. But what is he going to do about it? What does it mean?

Jesus was in the outback, *with the wild beasts*, and angels tended to him. With the wild beasts! Matthew and Luke didn't bother to copy that detail. Jesus spent Lent with animals and angels, overcoming his temptations, and learning to be true to who he was.

There in the outback- shaped by hours in the synagogue- he discovered the Good News. Simplicity itself! God was there. God was everywhere. At hand. Within reach. You could find God in the wilderness, not just in the synagogue or Temple.

And if God was within reach, people should do something about it!

> God is here!
> Believe it!
> Do something about it!

Jesus found a new story to tell, or perhaps he made sense of the old story in a new way. And because he knew who he was, he was not afraid to tell it.

What about us? You?

Who are you- and what story do you have to tell?

If you believe that the hidden Kingdom of God is right here, within reach, at hand, what have you done about it?

Lent 2 (Feb 25, 2024)

Salvation for the Jews.

Genesis 17:1-7, 15-16
Psalm 22:23-31
Romans 4:13-25
Mark 8:31-38 or Mark 9:2-9

The many voices in the Hebrew oral faith tradition were never harmonised into a single theology, even when edited into the written scriptures we have today. There is a majority "purist" view which condones violence, sexism and nationalist racism, and there are more universalist voices with a different opinion about who God is and how God relates to humanity. The story being read in churches all around the world this week – by over a billion people – definitely belongs in the nationalist racism category.

This bit from Genesis 17 is in the lectionary this week,

> "God said to Abram, "…I will give to you, and to your offspring after you, the land where you are now an alien, all the land of Canaan, for a perpetual holding; and I will be their God." Genesis 17:8)

Which would not be so bad if Canaan was *terra nullius*. Unfortunately, when the Jews finally arrive after their exodus from Egypt, that is clearly not the case,

"...when the LORD your God gives them over to you and you defeat them, then you must utterly destroy them. Make no Covenant with them and show them no mercy." (Deuteronomy 7:2)

What kind of salvation is being offered here? Who gets it, who misses out, what kind of God is described? This time the promise is to Abraham's descendants, a single race, though they have to go through slavery in Egypt before the great Exodus to the promised land.

The Exodus story is a powerful story of delivery from persecution, of salvation for those who are being treated unjustly. The Afrikaners referred to it constantly when they arrived in southern Africa. Those fleeing to the newly discovered Americas to avoid religious persecution in England saw that this story was their story.

God had guided them to the "Land of the Free." To a lesser extent, some white Christians arriving in Australian claimed the Exodus story, and the theme of deliverance to a promised land, as their story.

But to fill a *promised land*, one must deal with the Indigenous inhabitants, who don't just disappear. The Gumbaynggirr people where I live in Australia didn't just disappear. Nor did the Native Americans, the original Africans, or the Canaanites.

The book of Joshua records that the massacres happen, but not thoroughly enough for God's liking. The Israelites had to be divinely compelled to institute their "brown Israel policy,"

> "... if you turn back, and join the survivors of these nations left here among you, and intermarry with them, so that you marry their women and they yours, know assuredly that the LORD your God will not continue to drive out these nations before you... until you perish from this good land..." (Joshua 23:12-13)

In other words, if the Israelites faltered in their ethnic cleansing project, and intermarried rather than enslave and butcher, God would give up on them.

I cannot fathom how modern Christians can understand our faith as the continuation and fulfilment of this story. That somehow this violent, racist, story of deliverance and promise is part of *our* story, fulfilled in Jesus, and therefore worth telling during Lent. Should we abandon the story? No. We should keep it as a warning against the extremes of nationalism and religious zealotry, not repeat it uncritically in worship.

As a *warning* this story asks us,

Does God favour some people over others?

Do we?

Are some people simply objects to be disposed of?

Does God have no thought for Indigenous people?

Do we?

Humanity seems to be facing a raft of ecological and economic crisis, with corresponding political and social ones. Australia is one of the least affected countries, but we won't be forever, and growing numbers of us are already feeling the pinch. How are we hoping to get out of it? What "salvation" are we seeking? Is it sufficient if *our* nation, or *our* kind of people make it, at the expense of others?

The Israelites' salvation cost the Canaanites everything.

White Australia's "salvation" cost the Aboriginal people almost everything. What does our salvation now cost others?

Shall we also construct a story that lets us off the hook, in which everyone else is merely a bit part in the play in which we star? If not, what *is* our story, what deliverance are we hoping for? Not just for us, but for the world?

Let us flick back to Abraham. Even if his descendants didn't baulk from their divinely mandated ethnic cleansing, there was yet one more condition,

> "This is my Covenant, which you shall keep, between me and you and your offspring after you for every generation: Every male among you shall be circumcised… when he is eight days old… Any male who is not circumcised by cutting off the flesh of his foreskin shall be cut off from his

people; *he has broken my Covenant."* (Genesis 17:9-14)

The sign of salvation, by which you get to be part of this promise from Abraham through Joshua, is the cutting off of the end of your penis. Now that's just weird. Those babies whose parents baulk at *cutting off* their foreskins will be *cut off* from their people. They are out! And, so the story goes, this is to go on *for ever*.

An anonymous nurse unwittingly entered me into the Covenant when I was two days old, against my mother's wishes, but most Christians don't go in for penis pruning anymore. And when it was popular in the last century, it was for "hygiene" or to curb masturbation[1], not to keep their children Christian.

Jesus' disciple Peter, a Jew, had a vision that circumcision wasn't a requirement for entry into the Christian community (Acts 10-11).

---

[1] See John, J. *Christian Sex Today, lessons from Moses, Paul, Jesus and Darwin.*

But so clear were his holy scriptures on this point, and so strong was the tradition, and so harshly did the other Jewish Christians criticise him, that he wavered on the point, so that Paul, another Jew, had to confront him and force the issue (Galatians 2:11-14).

Eventually the other Jesus followers, also Jews, acknowledged that men *could* be a Christian, part of the "saved," without cutting off the end of their penis. Not only that, but amongst Christians no distinction was to be made between men and women, who didn't have foreskins to chop off in the first place (Galatians 3:28).

This was really, *really* radical! For a Jew to claim to be part of the saved community, yet keep his foreskin, was *completely unscriptural*. Everyone knew it, which is why it caused so much controversy. Just as radical was saying that "in Christ" there was no distinction between women and men.

Everyone knew that men were superior, as other parts of the Christians Scriptures make clear (1 Corinthians 11ff, 14:33ff; 1Timothy 2:11ff).

The first Christians were indisputably unbiblical!

Are *we* willing to be as unbiblical as the first Christians were, if that is where the Spirit is leading us?

Jesus probably grew up learning that those foreskin keeping gentiles were of little interest to God. How did he escape his inherited racism? In Mark it appears to be his conflict with the Syrophonecian woman (Mark 7). In Matthew, the Roman Centurion (Matthew 8). In Luke, written by a gentile, Jesus' cosmopolitan worldview is there from his very first speech in the synagogue, in which he claims that God loves foreigners. His audience is so incensed that they try to murder him (Luke 4).

Whenever he got the insight, by chapter eight of Mark, which includes this week's lectionary reading, Jesus is out amongst the Gentiles teaching and feeding four thousand of their men. Oh yes, plus women and kids.

What does the feeding of the 4000 mean?

Was it a real live miracle? Was it proof that God used to be able to make food out of thin air, but for some reason doesn't bother anymore, despite the billions of starving people in the world?

The hard bit for me in believing that it was a bona fide miracle isn't actually believing the miracle, but understanding why God has stopped feeding the hungry, if it's so easy.

Was the feeding a demonstration that salvation comes when people, seeing others share, start sharing themselves? Did one or two people start to do the right thing, and inspire others by their example? Did enough people get out the bits of food which they had stashed on them, to help feed everyone else? Was it like when we all pitch in after a flood to help muck out each other's houses? Was the miracle that people, inspired by listening to Jesus, actually loved their neighbour like he'd been telling them to? That those with food did for others as they would want done for them?

Or was the story a non-historical metaphor? A revelation of the shocking truth that salvation and wholeness, God's Kingdom, is offered *outside* the proper places? That it is offered to the wrong kinds of people?

Is it a declaration that God doesn't follow the rules?

How we answer those questions affects how we live now.

If we believe it was a magic miracle, we might pray that God will start magically creating bread again to feed the world, especially since it would really help with recruitment to our cause. Many prayers I hear in churches are, "God, please do something (magical) about problem X, Y and Z)."

If we take the second approach, we might commit to leading by example, sharing our bread and so inspiring others to share also, and build the Kingdom together. There are a wealth of other teachings of Jesus which suggest, or even compel us to follow, this approach. Doing so will bring us into conflict with those who want to make us fear our neighbour, and keep our bread for ourselves, so that we are easier to control.

Taking the third approach, we might risk breaking the rules ourselves. Doing the "wrong" things, in the "wrong" place, and the "wrong" way, for the "wrong" people. Like God and Jesus and the first Christians did.

Remembering that this will bring us into conflict with those who strive, like Joshua and later Christians, to stay pure, respectable, and law abiding. It will mean conflict with those who want us to keep our bread for the right kind of people.

Lent 3 (March 3, 2024)

Salvation for the obedient, merciless Jews.

Exodus 20:1-17
Psalm 19
1 Corinthians 1:18-25
John 2:13-22

We will follow the main Hebrew story – the story of the xenophobic Covenant between God and "his people"- for one more week, before turning to some of the Hebrew voices which undermine it.

All around the world today, the churches are reading the delivery of the Ten Commandments by God, through Moses, to the liberated community in the desert, on the way to their entry into, and ethnic cleansing of, Canaan.

People often feel compelled to admit that they don't go to church when they find out I'm a minister. Rather than admit that they find church boring, irrelevant, too early, too alienating, or just too wrong, they usually say that they really should go to church more often, but never explain why. Almost immediately this is followed by reassuring comments about the Ten Commandments, which they "believe in." I doubt many could recite them, but they certainly believe in them.

They may be shocked to know that the second commandment includes this reflection on the nature of God,

"I am a jealous God- *punishing children for the sins of parents*, to the third and fourth generation." (Exodus 20:5, Deuteronomy 5:9)

This may once have been a reasonable explanation of why people suffer when they have done nothing wrong, but is it an explanation we want to cling to today?

Do we want to keep it as part of the modern Christian story?

Has God kept a ledger of my great, great, great grandfather's evil deeds during the white invasion of Australia, for which I am now being punished?

Will God torture my great great, great grandchildren because of what I do?

And to add to the confusion, God continues by asserting his steadfast love to the thousandth generation of those who love him and keep his commandments. So, if I'm lucky enough to be descended from a faithful Israelite who was there on the day Moses came down the mountain, does that cancel out my wicked great, great, great grandfather?

I agree with whomever wrote Exodus that things *do* happen for a reason, and often the consequences of an action aren't felt by the perpetrators, but instead by innocent victims, even future generations.

But these bad things don't happen because God is still grumpy. Climate Change is an obvious example of people suffering for the (in)actions of previous generations. But there is not a direct lineal curse as in Exodus. Instead, the actions of rich people in one part of the world lead to consequences for poor people especially in other parts of the world. Aboriginal people today suffer the effects of racism going back generations, and would continue to suffer that legacy even if Australia was suddenly, miraculously, turned non-racist today. Again, it is not their Aboriginal ancestors, but the ancestors of others who laid the groundwork for their suffering.

But climate chaos has well understood scientific explanations, and racism has sociological ones.

Blaming that kind of suffering on God's intergenerational wrath makes no sense anymore. Good News that is grounded in the bad news of God's intergenerational wrath, as it is if we take the Ten Commandments as an accurate portrayal of the nature of God, also makes no sense.

The gospel ought to be able to say something about intergenerational ecological, political and social consequences. We could hear God warning us that our actions will affect future generations, and calling us to repent. But to imagine that God is the *cause* of those consequences must be abandoned in a scientifically, and we might hope morally, literate society.

Moving on from the first Ten Commandments of our jealous God, we get to the other hundred or so, including some real doozies,

> "When a slaveowner strikes a male or female slave with a rod and the slave dies immediately, the owner shall be punished. But if the slave survives a day or two, there is no punishment; for the slave is the owner's property. (Exodus 21:20)"

In this new community, which itself only just escaped the horrors of slavery in Egypt, slavery will continue, but this time with the Israelites as masters. And not particularly socially conscious ones at that.

The list of Laws is repeated on the eve of the crossing over into the "promised land", with the reminder that God's deal of deliverance/salvation is only valid if,

> "When the LORD your God brings you into the land that you are about to enter and occupy, and he clears away many nations before you, and when you defeat them, then you must utterly destroy them." (Deuteronomy 7:1ff)

In this new, divinely delivered community of faith which is called to be God's light to the nations (Isaiah 42:1-10), life is to continue pretty much as usual. Men own everything, including Jewish women and foreigners, and other animals will continue to be sacrificed because apparently God can't just forgive people, he needs something to die, even if it is a creature totally unrelated to the offence.

I must confess something.

I'm beginning to feel like I'm flogging a dead horse, going on and on about how unacceptable various offers of salvation are. And I'm feeling very naughty, like some kind of teenage rebel who delights in undermining authority- in this case God's or the Bible's.

When I sit back and reflect though, it is just so confronting, once you start replacing the question- "What's nice about this story?" (rainbows, babies being born to old people, delivery from slavery) with "What is being offered in this story, to whom, and by what sort of God?"

It is so confronting when we start to ask, "Who misses out in this story?"

It really troubles me that some people could think that God is the kind of God represented in these lectionary stories, which churches around the world are reading together. That these are good stories, part of the Good News. That it doesn't matter about the humans and other animals who are excluded.

Especially because, to a large degree, the church has by sleight of hand claimed that these offers of salvation are for us. Many Christians claim that *we* are now Abraham's people, the people of the Covenant. The new Covenant admittedly, but this new Covenant is seen as a spiritual *continuation or culmination* of, rather than a *repudiation* of, the original one.

Matthew in particular interpreted Jesus as the *fulfilment* of the Law, and this is a common Christian assumption today. Jesus is the fulfilment of this whole story from Abraham to Joshua. Not one dot or comma of the Law will pass away. In many churches, the story is that most of the Jews of Jesus' day rejected him, they are out, and we are in. Ignoring the need for circumcision and a few other crucial clauses, we have taken over the exclusive offers of salvation and flipped the Hebrew xenophobic scriptures into anti-Semitic ones in John's gospel and even Matthew (Matthew 27:24-26).[2]

---

[2] In contrast, Paul agrees that the original community has been temporarily rejected, but he is confident that somehow this is part

Should we just ditch these stories then?

No. We need to keep reminding ourselves just how misguided, selfish and illogical people of faith can be, just how badly we can misrepresent God in our own interests, and just how blind we can be to the harm we cause to those who are left out of the promises.

A few years back the political darling of American Right-Wing "Christianity" promised to build a wall to keep people out of their promised land, and if he stays out of gaol, he might be back again soon. Certainly, the kinds of inward looking, xenophobic, racist versions of salvation which got him into office, remain.

Is Jesus really the fulfilment of these biblical stories of murdered slaves, animal butchery, ethnic cleansing and male domination?

What did Jesus himself think? There is no single answer to that in the New Testament, and untangling what Jesus thought, from what his biographers and Paul

---

of yet another divine plan to make them jealous, and eventually welcome them back (Romans 10-11).

thought *about* him is a tricky business, judging by the number of books written on the subject.

But since this year the church is focussing on Mark's gospel, here's a clue from Mark. Notice that when the disciples hear the clue, they are far from impressed. If you read how Matthew rewrites this story, you will see that he was far from impressed too.

Jesus and his followers have just returned from the feeding of the four thousand, which, significantly for us, was performed outside Israel, in the land of the Greek foreskin keepers.

> "Jesus went on with his disciples to the villages of Caesarea Philippi; and on the way he asked his disciples, "Who do people say that I am?"
>
> And they answered him, "John the Baptist; and others, Elijah; and still others, one of the prophets." He asked them, "But who do you say that I am?" Peter answered him, "You are the Messiah."

And Jesus rebuked them, ordering them not to tell anyone about him." (Mark 8:27-30)[3]

Peter has just said that Jesus is the Messiah, the Christ, the long-awaited fulfilment of God's offer to the chosen race. The culmination of the Covenant- the dawning of their salvation.

And Jesus rebukes him and tells him to shut up!

According to all that Peter and the other disciples expected of the Messiah, according to how the story is meant to end, Jesus *is not* the Messiah. He is not the Christ they were expecting. Jesus goes on to talk, not about the Christ, but about the Son of Man, and his suffering.

Matthew cannot tolerate this. He is adamant that Jesus is the fulfilment of the Law, the Messiah, the new Moses.

---

[3] The NRSV says "sternly warned" but in most passages the Greek word is translated 'rebuke'

When Simon Peter answers Jesus' question, Matthew has Jesus say,

"*Blessed* are you, Simon son of Jonah! For flesh and blood has not revealed this to you, *but my Father in heaven*." (Matthew 16:17)

Did Jesus rebuke Peter, or congratulate him for being in tune with God?

More on that after God kills a few more people, this time for grumbling, or perhaps just for being very tired and hungry.

Lent 4 (March 10, 2024)

Salvation for compliant Jews.

Numbers 21:4-9
Psalm 107:1-3, 17-22
Ephesians 2:1-10
John 3:14-21

Let's get straight into the bible,

> "...Israel made a vow to the LORD and said, "If you will indeed give this people into our hands, then we will utterly destroy their towns." The LORD listened to the voice of Israel, and handed over the Canaanites; and they utterly destroyed them and their towns; so the place was called Hormah.
>
> From Mount Hor they set out by the way to the Red Sea, to go around the land of Edom; but the people became impatient on the way. The people spoke against God and against Moses, "Why have you brought us up out of Egypt to die in the wilderness? For there is no food and no water, and we detest this miserable food."
>
> Then the LORD sent poisonous serpents among the people, and they bit the people, so that many Israelites died. The people came to Moses and said,

"We have sinned by speaking against the LORD and against you; pray to the LORD to take away the serpents from us."

So Moses prayed for the people. And the LORD said to Moses, "Make a poisonous serpent, and set it on a pole; and everyone who is bitten shall look at it and live." (Numbers 21)

Numbers 21 starts with yet more divinely mandated ethnic cleansing of the Canaanites, as a part of God's plan of salvation for the Jews.

But now salvation is not even for all of the Jews! After the victory, some of them dare to complain that they starving. God responds, not with Manna or a feeding of the four thousand, but with another massacre, this time using poisonous serpents. Unsurprisingly, the masses fall into line rapidly, in the face of this God who keeps his beloved people under control by killing them so gruesomely.

Does killing people who dare to complain with snakes sound petty? Well, it gets even worse. A colleague far more versed in Hebrew than I am (a low bar, admittedly), points out that accusing the Israelites of being impatient is an unfair translation.

A better translation is that they had "reached the limit of their endurance," and were utterly discouraged. Elizabeth Raine concludes, "This is a people who are utterly tired, completely discouraged and at the end of their tether – 'impatient' doesn't begin to accurately describe their condition, and neatly lifts the blame for what follows from God onto the people." Elizabeth has been vindicated in that the very latest version of the NRSV replaces impatient with discouraged. It is somewhat mollifying that in Exodus 16-18, which tells the same story, God instead gives the people as much meat, food and water as they can eat! But back to Numbers and the lectionary.

God's offer of wholeness and liberation and salvation has narrowed from all men (through Noah), to Jewish men (through Abraham), to *compliant* Jewish men.

If this was a story of a husband and wife, as God and the people of faith are described by Isaiah, Ezekiel and Hosea, and later Ephesians, we would surely think of domestic violence. We would surely support and encourage the woman to leave. We, I hope, would no longer simply advise her not to grumble next time, or make him angry. To try harder to please him. To *comply and endure*.

To our great shame, I know that is precisely what some women *have* been told, and even *are* being told, and that stories like these maintain a culture in which that is possible.

It is not only this story from Numbers which is so dangerous, but also John's retelling of it in his gospel, which continues to be read in churches around the world today,

> "... *just as* Moses lifted up the serpent in the wilderness, so must the Son of Man be lifted up, that whoever believes in him may have eternal life... Those who believe in him are not condemned;

but those who do not believe are condemned already..." (John 3:14-17)

According to John, God is going to kill everyone who does not believe, just as God killed all those grumbling Israelites. Only those who look to the Serpent (who believe in Jesus) will be healed. It's no longer enough to *comply*, you must *believe*.

So the God who is offering me, a Christian, salvation, intends to kill every one of my friends and family who do not believe in Jesus, just like those grumbling Jews in the desert. And why not? This same God over the last few weeks has been shown to be willing to murder almost everyone on the planet (Noah), and then entire nations (Abraham and Joshua), and even the faithful if they dare grumble.

To be fair, it makes perfect sense that the first disciples, all of whom were Jewish, used the sacred stories they grew up with to try to understand this new thing God was doing in Jesus.

Matthew in particular goes to great pains, and selectively quotes and misquotes from a variety of bible texts, to show how Jesus is part of this story, and fulfils it. How he was the Messiah, the Christ, the anointed one of the people of those stories.

Years ago, I moved from being a Christian literalist who thought I had to accept all of those ancient Jewish stories too, to being a Conservative Evangelical who knew I could not, but struggled to justify the selectivity employed by my peers and mentors when declaring some texts (about gays) immutable, and others (about mass genocide, or wealth) needing contextuality.

Now I believe that it is essential for all Christians to categorically reject the image of God being portrayed in these stories, rather than repeating them (somewhat sanitised) in church.

What surprised me was that Jesus seemed to agree.

Let's revisit Mark 8:29-38

Peter and the disciples called Jesus the Christ.

Jesus *rebuked* them, telling them to shut up about him. He talked instead about the Son of Man.

Yet the very first line of Mark opens,

> "The beginning of the good news of Jesus Christ, the Son of God."

Look again though. It seems like Mark is using "Christ" as a last name, to identify him, much like Paul does, rather than as a description of what he was. He is not Jesus *the* Christ so much as Jesus Christ, *the Son of God*.

And in rebuking Peter, I suspect that Jesus was not just trying to keep his messianic identity secret, but emphatically declaring that Peter was wrong- Jesus was not the Jewish Messiah, the deliverer of Israel, the final stage in the story of Abraham and Moses and Joshua. He is the suffering Son of Man who will be vindicated in the last days.

These last days were probably understood by Mark to be heralded by the obliteration of the Jewish Temple and Jerusalem in 70AD.

"Then he began to teach them that the Son of Man must undergo great suffering, and be rejected by the elders, the chief priests, and the scribes, and be killed, and after three days rise again. He said all this quite openly. And Peter took him aside and began to rebuke him. But turning and looking at his disciples, he rebuked Peter and said, "Get behind me, Satan! For you are setting your mind not on divine things but on human things." (Mark 8:31)

So strong is the disciple's negative reaction to what Jesus says about suffering that Peter dares to rebuke Jesus, his teacher, and the one he has just called Christ! So emphatic is Jesus about what he is saying that he rebuked Peter right back, even calling him Satan!

Peter's mind is on human things.

Humans expect deliverance and victory over enemies. Humans expect the kind of salvation we've been reading about: the victory of some over others, winners and losers, the in crowd and the dregs, heroes and villains, saints and sinners, us and them. Jesus thinks that God sees it differently.

Jesus then goes on to describe what *he* thinks God is offering. It is not an offer to be found, but lost! To *lose* in order to win...

> "He called the crowd with his disciples, and said to them, "If any want to become my followers, let them *deny themselves and take up their cross* and follow me. For those who want to save their life will lose it, and those who lose their life for my sake, and for the sake of the gospel, will save it. For *what will it profit them to gain the whole world* and forfeit their life? Indeed, what can they give in return for their life? *Those who are ashamed of me and of my words* in this adulterous and sinful generation, of them the Son of Man will also be ashamed when he comes in the glory of his Father with the holy angels." (Mark 8:34-38)

Don't be ashamed.

Don't cling to success.

Don't look for victory.

All three offers were very counter cultural, then and now.

"For what will it profit them to gain the whole world and forfeit their life/soul/psyche?" (Mark 8:36)

Is *our* life being diminished because of something we are fixated on gaining? Have we given in to the daily crush of junk mail and consumerism, or been paralysed by a fear of scarcity which forces us to abandon our neighbours and focus on number one? To be a Noah building an ark for us and ours, and screw everyone else? What did it profit us to gain three jumbo packs of loo paper? What did it cost?

Jesus is offering us not the gain we seek, but the salvation we *need*, from whatever it is we are fixated by.

Perhaps we need salvation from belief in a God who builds a Kingdom through murder and bullying and threatening to kills us or hurt our children if we step out of line.

Perhaps we need instead an offer of salvation through the Spirit of the God whose Kingdom is right here within reach, for which we will suffer not because *God* makes us suffer, but because others prefer the world as it is, and have the power to keep it that way. For now.

Lent 5 (March 17, 2024)

*Spiritual Communism:
Jeremiah and Jesus*

Jeremiah 31:31-34
Psalm 51:1-12 or Psalm 119:9-16
Hebrews 5:5-10
John 12:20-33

We now hear from Jeremiah, who predicted the fall of Jerusalem and exile into Babylon, and writes to the Jewish middle and upper classes who have been deported,

> "The days are surely coming, says the LORD... when people shall no longer say: "The parents have eaten sour grapes, and the children's teeth are set on edge." But all shall die for their own sins.

The days are surely coming, says the LORD, when I will make a new Covenant with the house of Israel and the house of Judah. *It will not be like the Covenant that I made with their ancestors* when I took them by the hand to bring them out of the land of Egypt -- a Covenant that they broke.
But this is the Covenant that I will make with the house of Israel after those days, says the LORD: *I will put my law within them*, and I will write it on their hearts; and I will be their God, and they shall be my people.

No longer shall they teach one another, or say to each other, "Know the LORD," for they shall all know me, from the least of them to the greatest.

The day is surely coming, says the LORD, when Jerusalem shall be rebuilt…

It shall never again be uprooted or overthrown." (Jeremiah 31).

Over two thousand years later, this all sounds so sweet when we read it in church, and of course we assume that Jeremiah is talking about *us*, the spirit filled Christians who know God.

But this isn't a sweet passage. It's "I told you so." And not only that, Jeremiah is saying, in a nutshell, "all you priests and rulers who didn't listen to me should know that God is going to take us back to Jerusalem one day, and this time you won't be in charge: you will be obsolete, because we will all know God without your help, thank you very much!"

This is spiritual communism.

I suggested in the last chapter that Jesus rejected the old Covenants, which saw God building a Kingdom through violence and exclusion. Apparently, centuries before Jesus, the old Covenants were *already* being rejected by Jeremiah and others. The books of Ruth and Jonah, for example, reject the nationalistic impulse in the dominant stories of salvation.

Around the same time that Jeremiah is writing, the priests he confronts are busy compiling all of the oral traditions into the written stories we now have from Genesis through to the Exodus. All the stories of salvation (Noah, Abram, Exodus) were refashioned into one big story in Babylon.

The priests are shoring up the faith of a depressed people in exile, and probably shoring up their own position amongst the people, in the absence of access to the Temple. The books they compile in exile entrench the Law, make the Temple the centre point of the religion, along with its sacrificial system, and entrench their leadership of it.

So who do we listen to? Who convinces you? The priests with the written Law and Covenant based on ethnic purity, violence and obedience enforced by divinely appointed hierarchy? Or Jeremiah with his alternative Covenant, where people relate directly to God and have no need of priests?

If you aren't an ordained minister like me, you might be less compromised in your answer!

Are you convinced by the system or the rebel? The reformers or the revolutionaries?

Jeremiah's vision of divine rebellion against the priests' *status quo* was spectacular. It was also spectacularly incorrect.

After the return to Jerusalem the religious teachers remained. The Law was written on paper, not hearts, and the priests and teachers of the law remained until Jesus' day. Jewish Rabbis remain today, and Anglican, Roman Catholic and Orthodox priests have replaced Jewish ones.

The restored Temple was not "everlasting," but was obliterated by Rome shortly after Jesus' death. Contrary to Jeremiah's proclamation, it was both uprooted *and* overthrown.

Let us go back to Mark's story of Jesus, who continues Jeremiah's tendency to turn things on their head. Those who are last will be first. Those who lead must serve. If Jesus had a hierarchy, it was upside down. He offers salvation which involves humbling and demotion, not glory and power.

After catching the disciples arguing,

> "Jesus asked them what they were arguing about. But they were silent, for on the way they had argued with one another who was the greatest. He sat down, called the twelve, and said to them, "Whoever wants to be first must be last of all and servant of all."" (Mark 9:33-35)

Jesus went head-to-head against those who were *not* willing to be humbled, with those who were quite happy to be at the top of the hierarchy.

Here again he followed Jeremiah against the prevailing Temple system. The kings, the religious leaders, the bosses of the Temple cannot be trusted and need to be thrown out, as do the profiteers they allow to fill the Temple court,

> "Jesus and the disciples came to Jerusalem. And Jesus entered the Temple and began *to drive out* those who were selling and those who were buying in the Temple, and he overturned the tables of the money changers.
>
> He said, "Is it not written, 'My house shall be called a house of prayer for all the nations'? But you have made it a den of robbers." (Mark 11:15ff)

Then Jesus gets into several arguments with the religious leaders, telling the parable of the vineyard, which was a metaphor for Israel in his day. In the story, the true owner (God) sends messenger after messenger (the prophets) to the tenants (chief priests) to ask them to pay the rent they owe. But the tenants kill them all. Jesus continues,

"Finally, the owner sent his beloved son. They seized him, killed him, and threw him out of the vineyard. What then will the owner of the vineyard do? He will come and destroy the tenants and *give the vineyard to others.*"

When the chief priests realized that he had told this parable *against them,* they wanted to arrest him, but they feared the crowd. So they left him and went away." (Mark 12:1ff)

You don't call the elite murderous robbers without inviting retribution.

Jeremiah said that God would put the Law within people, so they wouldn't need the religious leaders to teach it to them. It didn't make him popular. Jesus said in the parable of the vineyard that the priests and scribes were to be replaced by others, since they kept killing the prophets like Jeremiah rather than listening to them. We all know how popular that was!

So, it seems that as Mark tells it, Jesus is following Jeremiah in *repudiating* the old covenants, the old promises, the old ways of understanding salvation. He is rejecting hierarchies, new and old.

And we have, in Mark at least, a clear understanding that Jesus died because the people he railed against had more political clout than he did.

Yet many Christians at this time of year will sing songs about how Jesus died because God wanted him to. They will say this coming Friday is *Good* Friday because it was the day God killed Jesus instead of killing us. Jesus was the perfect sacrifice that replaced all the millions of imperfect sacrifices which Jews had long made to God. Jesus took the final punishment which we all deserved.

Rather than killing all of us, as God should have, and as he did in the days of Noah, God killed Jesus the God-man.

Yet let us turn to the Synoptic gospels. That is, Mark, and Luke and Matthew, who both adapt Mark's stories and add some of their own. Jesus says nothing about being a new sacrifice, or a new high priest, or any kind of channel for our forgiveness.

Even Matthew, who was keen to affirm the validity of the old Covenants, records Jesus placing himself in the tradition of Jeremiah, Amos and Micah, who claimed that God desires mercy, *not* sacrifice. (Matthew alone does add to Jesus' words concerning the wine of the last supper, "poured out for many (not all) for the forgiveness of sins")

Since Jesus thought that God desired mercy, not sacrifice, why do so many Christians think he *was* a sacrifice?

Because it's *biblical*. It's very much in the epistle to the Hebrews, and very much in Paul. There is even a hint of it in John's gospel.

In John, however, written much later than the other gospels, we are reading theology *about* Jesus, put on his lips, rarely if ever his actual words or deeds.[4]

This idea of Jesus' sacrificial atoning death is biblical. It is also *unbiblical*. It is not in Mark, Matthew or Luke. Luke also wrote Acts, which does say that God had Jesus' death planned all along, but not that it was a sacrificial death.

Who is right?

We either admit the two points of view and choose one, or pretend that there is only one point of view and gloss over the other.

It is overwhelmingly more likely that the synoptic gospels hold the more accurate picture of what Jesus thought his life was all about, and how he thought we were made right with God, than John or Paul do.

---

[4] For one thing, contrast his long, third person monologues in John with the content of the Synoptic gospels.

If so, Jesus did not see himself as a divinely appointed sacrifice for our sins on our behalf. As a Christian, or maybe a Jesusian, I'm going to go with his vision of God and the Kingdom.

So at least half of the Easter songs we sing are completely wrong. Which is a shame because some of their tunes are so great, even for a generation Xer like me! The first one off the top of my head is *How Great Thou Art*, which opens with magnificent poetry about God's awesomeness and presence throughout the universe and our Earth, but then sums up the whole significance of Jesus life, not by recalling his teaching or actions like the gospel writers would have, but by going with Paul and saying that it is all about God killing Jesus instead of me,

> "And when I think that God,
> His Son not sparing;
> Sent Him to die,
> I scarce can take it in;
> That on the Cross,
> My burden gladly bearing,
> He bled and died

To take away my sin."
(How Great Thou Art, verse 3)

I am as sure as I can be that this is not how Jesus understood salvation.

Not because I'm a squeamish liberal who doesn't like the idea of being, "washed in the blood of the lamb," or the thought of God torturing my unbelieving family and friends for eternity.

I don't think Jesus would sing verse three of *How Great thou Art*, because of what he said two thousand years ago, at least according to the Synoptic writers.

Lent 6 (Mar 24, 2024)

Salvation outside the Temple

Palm Sunday

Psalm 118:1-2, 19-29
Mark 11:1-11

To recap the last days of Jesus' story, in Mark's gospel:

Jesus came to Jerusalem and was infuriated when he saw the Temple and its system for the first time. During his outback retreat he realised that Jeremiah was at least partly right: God was at hand, and everyone could just reach out and grasp the Kingdom. He'd lived that experience for a year as he travelled and proclaimed this Kingdom. Calling people to believe it and do something about it. To repent-and change their ways.

Here in the centre of Judaism, here at the Temple, he saw barrier after barrier standing between people and God. Gentiles were banished to the outer court of the Temple. Jewish women had to stay in the outer room. Even men weren't allowed into the inner holy of holies where God's presence was said to reside.

In the Temple, the Kingdom was *not* within reach.

And whichever room they were allowed into, people first had to purchase animals for sacrifices to hope to access this Kingdom. Poor widows were giving everything they had to be made right with God, according to the system of sacrifices and Temple tithes (Mark 12:38-44).

The priestly system was getting in the way of people and God. Jesus drew on the traditions of prophets like Micah, Amos and Jeremiah, declaring that God desired mercy, not sacrifice, and that God was with people – directly, at hand- with no more need for priests or sacrifices to mediate God to them.

The Kingdom is at hand! You need no mediator! Hot on the heels of his protest against the selling of sacrificial animals in the Temple court, Jesus tells the disciples how to be right with God, and it has nothing to do with the Temple or the sacrifice either of animals or himself,

> "Whenever you stand praying, forgive, if you have anything against anyone; *so that your Father in heaven may also forgive you your trespasses.*" (Mark 11:25)

This is the outworking of his summary of the Law into two commandments,

"The first is, 'Hear, O Israel: the Lord our God, the Lord is one; you shall love the Lord your God with all your heart, and with all your soul, and with all your mind, and with all your strength.' The second is this, 'You shall love your neighbour as yourself.' There is no other commandment greater than these." (Mark 12:28ff)

When a scribe accepted that these two commandments were more important than animal sacrifices, Jesus assured him that he is not far from the Kingdom.

In Mark, the events of Easter are the consequence of Jesus declaring that having a right relationship with God is something we can *do ourselves*, for free, with no mediator or sacrifice, right now!

Or if there is a sacrifice, the sacrifice is to forgive others. That's it. Sound too easy? Try doing it!

Perhaps it is not surprising that Jews preferred to buy a sacrifice to pay for forgiveness. Or that the church did such a roaring trade selling pardons and indulgences before the Reformation.

Our world would crumble if the two billion Christians around the world took Jesus seriously on this. Maybe that was the idea.

According to Jesus, God's forgiveness of us is intertwined with our forgiveness of others. In Mark 11:25, Matt 6:11 and Luke 6:37 it *depends* on us forgiving others. Here Jesus is confronting those who presume they are forgiven and part of the in crowd, not heaping another burden on the backs of those who are abused or oppressed.

Given these explicit statements and stories, why is the most common Easter story about Jesus that he brings about our forgiveness *for us*! Placating God by dying in our place. The atoning sacrifice for our sins. The very *opposite* of what he is on about in the synoptics.

Why? Because Jesus' version is too bloody hard!

It is easier to follow Paul and the author of Hebrews. In their story, Jesus does the forgiveness stuff for us. He pays the price, and the divine scales are balanced. The sacrifice is made for us by Jesus, the perfectly obedient human (and in much later church tradition, the God-human), who has become the sacrificial lamb of God.

This is great. God is still in control. God planned the whole thing, violence is still the basis for maintaining a Covenant (this time violence against Jesus, not those Aboriginals in Canaan or whinging Jews or everyone except Noah), and NOTHING HAS REALLY CHANGED.

The church has simply replaced Israel as the people of the New Covenant. Which is the Old Covenant, with Jesus reprising the role of both sacrificial animal and sacrificing priest.

This was a really clever way for Jesus' Jewish disciples to make sense of the murder of Jesus, and the destruction of the Temple, given that they continued to experience God's ongoing presence amongst them.

Really try to imagine being a devout Jew, maybe a zealous ex-Pharisee like Paul or perhaps an ex-priest writing the letter to the Hebrews. Someone for whom the Temple and animal sacrifice were a centuries old, unquestioned pillars of your faith. Someone for whom the Jews were obviously the centre of the story of God and the world. Imagine when they meet someone who seems to them to be anointed- the Messiah - the hero who was promised to purify Israel and drive out the oppressors. Someone they see God at work in.

Imagine what happens when, instead of taking over the Temple and driving out the Romans, Jesus is condemned by the priests and butchered by the Romans. Butchered. Yet they discover, as we will soon see, that this isn't the end of his story! God has somehow prevailed. Butchered? No, maybe sacrificed! How else to explain Jesus' death except as part of the divine plan of the all-powerful God, the sacrifice to end all sacrifices. *That* must be why God used the Romans to destroy the temple in 70AD, you might conclude. God didn't lose, God won!

It is a miracle that *any* Jewish writing doesn't interpret Jesus as a sacrifice or the new high priest. Yet the synoptic gospels don't.

It is left to Paul, the zealous Pharisee, who never met Jesus in the flesh or heard his teaching, and who includes so little of Jesus' life in his writings, to start the "sacrificial lamb" theory. John, writing much later, does have John the Baptist proclaim the Lamb of God, who takes away the sin of the world! But this happens not so much through Jesus' sacrifice in our place, but mystically through eating his flesh and drinking his blood, and believing in him.

In none of the gospels does Jesus say anything like, "I will die so that God may forgive you."

He says, "*You* forgive others, *so that* God may forgive you." (Mark 11:25; Matt 6:11ff; Luke 6:37)

In Matthew, Jesus emphasises that God wants mercy, not sacrifice (Matt 9:13; 12:17).

If you want a healthy relationship with God, if you want to be forgiven, then forgive others. Be merciful, as God is merciful. Do not judge, and you will not be judged.

Jesus *does not* win our forgiveness in the synoptic gospels. He does not die to appease an angry or offended or "righteous" God.

Jesus *declares* the path to forgiveness and challenges people to follow it. The Kingdom of God is within reach- do something about it! (Mark 1:14; Matt 4:17)

Through his baptism, his outback retreat, his year of seeing the Kingdom manifest through him, Jesus is willing to die rather than keep silent about this truth: God desires mercy, and offers it apart from the Temple and its trappings. God always has.

This is Jesus' sacrifice. To get through the torment of Gethsemane, determined to proclaim and live the Kingdom to the end, trusting that it will not be the end after all.

A Christian is someone who *believes what Jesus said and demonstrated about God* and *does something about it* (repenting and forgiving), not someone who "believes in Jesus" as a way to avoid God's metaphorical poisonous snakes of destruction.

I would *so* prefer it to be about believing.

To go with Paul and Hebrews at Easter.

I really would.

But it is *biblical* to see Jesus as declaring a path to salvation for us, rather than somehow being that path. It is *gospel* to realise that he sacrificed himself on behalf of his vision of God, not that he was sacrificed *to* God. At least that's what he reckoned.

Let's try to follow the Way of Christ this Easter: Forgiving others, maybe forgiving ourselves, and opening ourselves up to divine forgiveness.

Let's be merciful, as God is merciful.

I pray that we will discover that despite the darkness in ourselves and others which we will soon acknowledge on Maundy Thursday; forgiveness, love and light cannot be killed off forever.

Maundy Thursday

(March 28, 2024)

Bad things happen to good people.

Even Jesus.

Exodus 12:1-4, (5-10), 11-14
Psalm 116:1-2, 12-19
1 Corinthians 11:23-26
John 13:1-17, 31b-35

Through Mark we are taken into the depths of Jesus' despair. Jesus has eyes to see and ears to hear God all around him and within him, and yet he knows darkness, despair, doubt and uncertainty. And he finds courage in the face of it.

We remember the disciples. Passionate people, who know confusion, anger, fear, greed, guilt and shame.

Maundy Thursday signifies the time when Jesus, having eaten a last meal with his friends, and possibly having washed their feet in a last desperate attempt to get them to understand what he is on about, takes them to a dark garden, where his fears nearly overwhelm him.

There's really no better option than to read the story in Mark, preferably alone and in the dark. If you need a soundtrack, a host of Gen-X songs come to mind (to me at least, being a Gen-Xer myself):

REM- everybody hurts; Sinead O'Connor- I do not want what I haven't got; Nick Cave- the weeping song; George Michaels, they won't go where I go; U2- end of the world; Isis- treat yourself gently. And maybe at the end, Sinead O'Connor- Guide me God.

Here's the story,

> "They went to a place called Gethsemane; and Jesus said to his disciples, "Sit here while I pray." He took with him Peter and James and John, and began to be *distressed and agitated*. And he said to them, "I am *deeply grieved, even to death*; remain here, and keep awake." And going a little farther, he *threw himself on the ground* and prayed that, if it were possible, the hour might pass from him. He said, "Abba, Father, for you all things are possible; remove this cup from me; yet, not what I want, but what you want." He came and found them sleeping; and he said to Peter, "Simon, are you asleep? Could you not keep awake *one hour*? Keep awake and pray that you may not come into the time of trial; the spirit indeed is willing, but the flesh is weak." And again he went away and prayed, saying the same words. And once more he came and found them sleeping, for their eyes were very heavy; and they did not know what to say to him. He came a third time and said to them, "Are you still sleeping and taking your rest? Enough!

The hour has come; the Son of Man is betrayed into the hands of sinners. Get up, let us be going. See, my betrayer is at hand." (Mark 14:32-42)

If you want a reading in addition to Mark, try *The Paradoxical Commandments,* by Kent M. Keith (1968), which includes the following,

> "People are illogical, unreasonable, and self-centred.
> Love them anyway.
> …
> If you do good, people will accuse you of selfish ulterior motives.
> Do good anyway.
> …
> What you spend years building may be destroyed overnight.
> Build anyway.
> …

Give the world the best you have and you may end up crucified for it.
Give the world the best you have anyway.[5]"

If you find yourself in a Garden of Gethsemane, with despair and darkness looming unbidden, and maybe even clinging to your soul through Friday and Saturday, remember not to stay there forever. Sunday's coming! But not quite yet.

---

[5] https://www.paradoxicalcommandments.com/ He doesn't say 'crucified'

Friday (March 29, 2024)

There is nothing good about it.

Isaiah 52:13-53:12
Psalm 22
Hebrews 10:16-25 or
Hebrews 4:14-16; 5:7-9
John 18:1-19:42

"Stop all the clocks, cut off the telephone,
Prevent the dog from barking with a juicy bone,
Silence the pianos and with muffled drum
Bring out the coffin, let the mourners come."

If I had permission, I'd put the whole poem here. It's all you need for Shitty Friday.

You can read the rest of *Funeral Poem*, by W. H. Auden at the British library online collection.

Resurrection Sunday (March 31, 2024)

The world's first cliff-hanger.

Acts 10:34-43 or Jeremiah 31:1-6
Psalm 118:1-2, 14-24
Colossians 3:1-4 or Acts 10:34-43
John 20:1-18 or Matthew 28:1-10

Easter Sunday, and what a confusing Sunday it is!

In Mark, Jesus gives no wonderful pep talk like he does in Matthew. There are no snacks and no promises of the Spirit as in Luke, or BBQ fish on the beach and breathing of the Spirit into the disciples like in John.

Instead, a young man, not even an angel, tells the women that Jesus isn't in the tomb- he has gone ahead of them to Galilee. Terrified and amazed, they flee the tomb, *saying nothing to anybody because they were so scared.*

The end.

Mark didn't want to know how the Resurrection worked, what it looked like, or even what was said afterwards. But what reader could be satisfied with that ending? Obviously, the women must have said *something* to *someone*, or Mark would never have been written!

What did they say?

Mark's abrupt ending pushes us back to his beginning, to the first words he records for Jesus, spoken - funnily enough - in Galilee,

"The time *is fulfilled*, the Kingdom of heaven has come near. Repent! (you disciples that fled the scene and deserted him, or you disciples reading this, who are tempted to desert him in the face of Roman persecution) and believe this good news!" (Mark 1:15)

The other gospel writers needed "better" endings. Proper endings where all the loose ends are tied up. Through various contradictory stories, and drawing on a cosmology which only made sense at the time, they all tried to get across the point that through the Resurrection, the mission of Jesus was continuing in his followers, because the Spirit of God was still with them and active amongst them.

The Resurrection *is still occurring in us*: John's living streams of the Spirit of compassion, peace, and forgiveness are burbling up within us: showing that the same Spirit which was in Jesus flows through us, allowing us collectively to do "greater things" than Jesus did. The Kingdom is still at hand. Jesus' murderers failed.

Thinking of the Resurrection as an ongoing reality, empowered by the streams of living water- the Spirit - isn't perfect. But it makes some sense at least, unlike tales of a physical body being reanimated and then flying up through the clouds (Luke 24:51, Acts 1:9).

The problem with Luke's account of Jesus' Resurrection is his reliance on outdated cosmology, more than the *possibility* or otherwise of physical Resurrection. We now know just how big those heavens which Jesus levitated into are. And we've been up there and didn't see him.

Even if Jesus travelled at the speed of light, he would still have between 1000 and 100,000 years to go before he got out of the Milky Way galaxy.

If heaven is a place "up there" then it is presumably at least as far away as the edge of our galaxy.

Of course, few literalists *literally* believe that Jesus is sitting somewhere out there in heaven. Yet many insist that we must believe that he *did* walk around in a new kind of body, which ate fish and had nail marks, and which did fly up into the clouds.

Far fewer of us literally believe the associated expectation of the first Christians, that our bodies will also *literally* reanimate at some point. We have gone off the bodily Resurrection idea in favour of the quite unbiblical "spiritual heaven" of the Greeks. And fair enough, with 100 billion people having been born so far, there's no room for all the bodies anymore. Who wants to live on an Earth that crowded, even a re-Edenised Earth? Let's guess that only 5% of humans make the grade and get into heaven. Who could enjoy paradise in the new Jerusalem with the noise of 95 billion people below them, screaming in everlasting torment? That would be 256 times louder than 1 person screaming.

What of literal historicity of the rest of the Resurrection stories? Did the disciples go to Galilee to find Jesus (as Mark and Matthew claim) or stay in Jerusalem (as Luke says)? Did Jesus breathe the Spirit into his followers (John 20:22) or did it fall upon them 50 days later (Acts 2)?

Let's not judge each other on how we make sense of these contradictory Resurrection stories. Everyone who does not literally believe that Jesus is a projectile zooming through space has dipped their toe into the possibility that the bodily Resurrection stories are not literal.

And that's before we get to the story, only in Matthew, of the zombie saints rising from the grave at the Resurrection and travelling into town (27:52ff). I've never heard that story mentioned at Easter time.

People like Michael Dowd have little interest in working out what actually happened to Jesus' body. He is more interested in working out what Resurrection *means*, since he thinks that was the point of the stories anyway: to convey meaning, not history. He finds the Resurrection not just on Easter Sunday, but archetypically throughout our lives, and indeed the universe,

> "I don't merely *believe* in the Resurrection. I *know* that for billions of years, chaos, death, and destruction have catalysed new life, new opportunities, and new possibilities. I know, both from my own life and from Earth's history, that Good Fridays are consistently followed by Easter

Sundays. The story of Christ's death and Resurrection reminds me of this. (Thank God for Evolution p. 188)"

I get his point, and the book is great.

But Friday isn't just a death, it's a *murder*. A deliberate decision by the Powers that Be to destroy the message of God's love for all, and of the last and least being first and greatest in God's Kingdom.

And Resurrection Sunday isn't only the common experience that things need to die to make way for new things, as we must die to make way for our grandchildren.

It is the claim that the bloke who was declared beloved at his baptism; driven into the outback by the Spirit, and who was properly understood only by the powers of evil; prevailed. His brutal murder failed, because the Resurrection is the fact that the same Spirit who empowered Jesus, empowers all of us to live out the truth as forgiven forgivers.

The time *is* fulfilled.
The Kingdom *is* within reach.
do something about it!

So, what are *you* "doing about it?"

Join the conversation at ecofaith.org

www.ingramcontent.com/pod-product-compliance
Lightning Source LLC
Chambersburg PA
CBHW020327010526
44107CB00054B/2013